Concert at a Railway Station

Osip Mandelstam

Concert at a Railway Station

—a selection of poems—

*translated from Russian
by Alistair Noon*

Shearsman Books

First published in the United Kingdom in 2018 by
Shearsman Books
50 Westons Hill Drive
Emersons Green
BRISTOL
BS16 7DF

Shearsman Books Ltd Registered Office
30–31 St. James Place, Mangotsfield, Bristol BS16 9JB
(this address not for correspondence)

www.shearsman.com

ISBN 978-1-84861-601-1

Translation copyright © Alistair Noon, 2018.

The right of Alistair Noon to be identified as the translator of this work
has been asserted by him in accordance with the
Copyrights, Designs and Patents Act of 1988.
All rights reserved.

Acknowledgements

Some of these translations have appeared previously, mostly in earlier versions, in *3AM Magazine, Asymptote, Black Herald, Blackbox Manifold, B O D Y, Cambridge Literary Review, Cerise, Circumference, Eyewear, Fortnightly Review, Four Centuries: Russian Poetry in Translation, Glasgow Review of Books, Grasp, Guernica, Horizon Review, Litter, Long Poem Magazine, Mayday, Molly Bloom, NOON: journal of the short poem, nth position, Ofi Press, Oxonian Review, Paris Lit Up, SAND, Shearsman, The Asses of Parnassus, The New Statesman, Truck, Washington Square Review* and *York Literary Review.*
Thanks to the editors concerned.

Contents

Translator's note	9

from *Stone*

The muffled sound of the fruit	13
Read only what children would read	14
Against the pale-blue enamel	15
No moon but a clock-face. How's it a sin	16
On Foot	17
Hagia Sophia	18
Notre Dame	19
Bach	20
In the quiet suburbs the porters	21
The Admiralty	22
Cinema	23
Dombey and Son	25
Poisoned bread, not a drop in the air	26
[Valkyries]	27
Let's rhyme about Rome, that city of wonders	28
"Ice cream!" Sun. The airy biscuits	29
Let the brief names of the flowering cities	30

from *Tristia*

A Menagerie	33
The night that can't be undone	35
Salamis, breath-taking island	36
The Decembrist	37
Our hostess had time to say a few words while the stream	38
[Meganom]	39
Tristia	41
As if we'd laid the sun in the ground	43
I miss mosquitoes in winter	45

from *Poems 1921–1925*

Concert at a Railway Station	49
One night, as I washed in the yard	50
Light Rain in Moscow	51
Century	52
The Man who Finds the Horseshoe	54
The Ode on Slate	57
Through the gypsy camp of the darkened street, I'll rush	60

from *New Verses*

What dreadful spot are we headed for now	63
Armenia	64
[Leningrad]	69
Like the bulk of a nation starting	70
Lamarck	71
Impressionism	73
To the German Language	74
We live, but feel no land at our feet	76

from *The Voronezh Notebooks*

from the *First Notebook*

I live in key kitchen gardens	79
Hey there, Earphones, Earphones you snitch!	80
Voronezh, Crow-Town, permit me to go	81
What street are we on?	82
Black Earth	83
You took away my seas, the run and the running jump	84
[The River Kama]	85
We're brimming with life, and that's capital	87
The full-weight ingots of Roman nights	88
St. Isaac's freezes to each dead eyelash	89

from the *Second Notebook*

The Birth of the Smile	90
I marvel at the kids and snow	91
Goldfinch friend, when I tilt my head	92
Today is kind of yellow-gobbed	93
Inside the mountain, the idol sits idly	94
[Core of an ocean, this region	95
The goldfinch goes into shudders	97
I feel the winter begin	98
It isn't cheap, this yeast	99
January. Where can I go to vanish?	100

from the *Third Notebook*

Verses on the Unknown Soldier	101
[Reims – Laon]	106
So that the sandstone, mate of the wind	107
I raise these leaves to my lips	108
[Verses to Natasha Shtempel]	109

Children's Poetry

Balloons	113
Ants	116
The Egg	117

Occasional and Joke Poems

From *An Anthology of Ancient Nonsense*	121
Baron Emil grabs a knife	121
[From Dmitri Shepelenko's album]	122
As if some prophet down from talking with the Lord	122
Natasha's back, but where's she been?	122
Oh Natasha, how clumsy of me	122
Decision	123

Uncollected Poems

So if our enemies took me captive   127
Should I take charcoal for the highest praises   128

Biographical note   132
Notes on the poems   137

Translator's note

The translations were originally made from the edition Osip Mandel'shtam, *Sochineniya v dvukh tomakh, Tom pervyi*, Moscow, Khudozhestvennaya literatura, 1990, compiled by P.M. Nerler, with notes by the latter and A.D. Mikhailov. They were reworked on the basis of A.G. Mets's 2009 edition, Osip Mandel'shtam, *Polnoe sobraniye sochinenii i pisem v tryokh tomakh, Tom 1*, Moscow, Progress-Pleyada. Despite numerous editors' and scholars' efforts, the authoritative text of many poems – in particular, the post-1930 poems almost entirely unpublished in Mandelstam's lifetime – remains unstable. This derives from uncertainties as to whether changes and variants resulted from deliberate artistic choices and revisions, (self-)censorship, concealment, miscopying, misdictation, the memorization process, false recollection at a much later date, and/or oral transmission, or lack of access to copies deposited with friends for safekeeping, or a combination of these, on the respective parts of both Osip Mandelstam and his wife Nadezhda Mandelstam, his *de facto* secretary while he was alive and plenipotentiary literary executor – at great personal cost to herself – after his death. As an indication of this textual instability and to facilitate comparison, some variants have been included in the main text placed in square brackets, where they represent additions, or in the notes where they are alternatives. The Mets edition has also been followed with regards to the naming of poems, omitting titles by which poems have subsequently become known but which were not Mandelstam's.

The selection and its title are the translator's. Notes have been largely kept to a minimum of what seems necessary to understand discrete references, without being exhaustive as to the background to the original poems' writing. Readers interested in the latter are referred, with regard to the later poems, to Richard and Elizabeth McKane's *The Moscow and Voronezh Notebooks* (Bloodaxe, 2003). Some non-exhaustive bibliographical information can also be found in the notes.

I am grateful for the critical work of scholars including Clarence Brown, Clare Cavanagh, Gregory Freidin, Mikhail Gasparov, Yuri Levin, Lada Panova, Andrew Reynolds, Omry Ronen, Olga Sedakova and Peter Zeeman, as well as to Ralph Dutli for his comprehensive biography of Mandelstam (in German; translations into Russian and French exist but none into English at the time of going to press). Thanks are also due to earlier and other current translators of Mandelstam, whose work has, among other things, provided me with an opportunity to cross-check my own interpretation of the originals; José Manuel Prieto's account of translating into Spanish the poem that has become known as 'The Stalin Epigram', and translated here as *'We live, but feel no land at our feet'*, was particularly helpful (http://www.bu.edu/translation/files/2011/01/Allen-Handout2.pdf, last accessed 2 September 2017). I am extremely grateful for the assistance provided to me by Iliya Bolotyansky, Vadim Erent, Alexander Filyuta, Ilia Kitup, Eugene Ostashevsky, Nadja Otten and Alexei Prokopiev in answering frequent and extensive queries, as well as to Kelvin Corcoran, Henry King, Andrew Reynolds, Justin Quinn, Emma Liggins, Antonia Maxwell, Christian Hawkey, Anthony Barnett and Antony Rowland for assistance, support, information and feedback, both major and minor, to Tony Frazer for his patience, also to Alan Baker and John Bloomberg-Rissman, and not least to Sabine Heurs, for putting up with several years of frequent distracted silence intermittently interrupted by mumblings in Russian and English. All shortcomings in the translations remain mine.

from

Stone

The muffled sound of the fruit
that carefully broke from a branch,
amid the incessant chant
of the silence deep in the woods…

1908

Read only what children would read,
and dream what children think matters;
once the great things lie scattered,
shake off grief and rise to your feet.

Existence exhausts me to death –
oh nothing it owns is of worth.
But I love this desolate earth:
I've never known any place else.

In that distant garden, I'd rock
on a wooden swing. I recall
how the spruces were dark and tall
in the delirium of the fog.

1908

Against the pale-blue enamel
that April makes conceivable,
the branches of birch trees will stand
and gradually ripen to evening.

Their pattern is sharp and complete,
that stiffened gauze is fine,
like a drawing that somebody's neatly
traced out on a plate of china.

Some merciful artist performs
a design on the glassy heavens,
knowing the transience of such force,
oblivious to the sorrow of death.

1909

No moon but a clock-face. How's it a sin
that while it dazzles my eyes I examine
the muted stars' milky light?

Poet Batyushkov,[1] son to a parson,
how he'd spout on. "What's the time?" they'd ask him.
"Eternity", he replied.

1912

On Foot

To M.L. Lozinsky [2]

Nearing mysterious mountain tops,
I can't defeat the fear I feel;
content with every swallow aloft,
I love how the bells rise into a peal.

I'm an ancient walker. A chasm reveals
a sagging bridge I approach and cross;
I think I can hear the snow uncongeal,
how the whole of time ticks on stone clocks.

But I'm no traveller whose name would stop
your eye on pages the light will steal.
There's a grief I sing but keep concealed.

The flying bells bear my soul off,
but avalanches roll in the hills for real.
No music pulls me back from the drop.

1912

Hagia Sophia

Hagia Sophia, where the Lord ordained
that the emperors and nations should halt,
that dome of yours hangs on a chain
from the heavens, observers report.

The centuries followed Justinian's lead
when, for the sake of gods that were foreign,
Ephesian Diana allowed him to steal
one hundred and seven green marble columns.

But what was your architect thinking
as he lavished out apses and recesses,
and with his intensity of spirit and vision
deployed them to the east and the west?

Sublime temple, afloat in the world,
your forty windows a triumph of light,
the four archangels on sails unfurled
in your dome are an even sublimer sight.

Outliving centuries, nations, topped
by a sphere, it's wise this building,
and the seraphim there and their echoing sobs
won't warp its dim-lit gilt.

1912

Notre Dame

A basilica stands where Roman justice
judged another nation: displaying its nerves,
as joyful as Adam to have stood there first,
the light cross-vault plays with its muscles.

But a secret scheme is revealed outside:
the strength of the saddling arches forestalls
the buckle and collapse of the laden walls,
and the war-ram of the bold vault stays idle.

Maze of the maker, forest to pass
understanding, the Gothic mind's abyss,
Egyptian force, the meekness of Christians,
oak beside reed where plumblines are tsars.

But what might I one day create,
stronghold *Notre Dame*, I'd think on my trips
to study and study those monstrous ribs:
a kind of beauty from hostile weight.

1912

Bach

The parishioners are children of dust,
no icons here but the boards
where the psalms of Johann Sebastian
are nothing but numbers in chalk.

What clashing voices reside
in disorderly pubs and cathedrals,
but Bach, you exult like Isaiah:
nobody trumps you in reason.

High-level squabbler, I guess
you found the mind good handrails
by holding hard to the evidence
when you played your grandkids chorales.

And sound? Old man, you're stubborn,
and none of those sixteenth portions
are anything more than your grumbling
in the polysyllabic organ.

Now, the Lutheran preacher
ascends to his pulpit's blackness
and mingles the din of his speeches
with yours, that would answer in anger.

1913

In the quiet suburbs the porters
are scraping away at the snow,
and the bearded peasants are walking
beside me along this road.

Women gleam in their headscarves,
the crazy mongrels are yapping,
and crimson roses on samovars
sparkle in houses and taverns.

1913

The Admiralty

In the northern capital, a poplar droops
its dusty leaves round a glasslike clock;
a frigate or acropolis gleam through that hoop,
siblings to sea and sky, far off.

Peter's descendants have drawn straight lines
by this mast you can't touch that castles the air:
beauty's no whim of the semi-divine
but whatever a carpenter's eye ensnares.

Four elements were gifts to us from on high,
but a free human being created a fifth.
Come on, let's agree that this ark denies
the expanse's dominance, chaste-built as it is.

Impulsive medusae hold on hard,
and anchors rust like ploughs cast aside.
Where the knots of a trio of dimensions part,
three streets file out onto global tides.

1913

Cinema

Three benches plus a projector.
The fever of sentimentality.
A posh heiress entangled
in her evil rival's nets.

Hands off this love's true flight,
our heroine's done nothing wrong!
Her love is pure, near-platonic,
for some lieutenant of the fleet,

sired on the side by a grey count.
Our officer wanders the desert,
and now the pretty countess's
comic strip gets off the ground.

She starts to wring her hands
like a gypsy gone insane.
The lovers split. Demonic sounds
pound from a hounded piano.

Her trust's not hard to abuse.
She possesses sufficient bravery
to swoop on some crucial papers
of interest to enemy HQs.

Along the chestnut boulevard
a black motor car lumbers.
The film reel rattles. A thump
of alarm thrills our hearts.

Sensibly dressed, with her *sac à voyage*,
she travels the roads and rails,
only scared of the bloke on her tail,
and gags at a dry mirage.

The finale's bitter and trite:
ends don't justify means!
He gets his dad's domains,
while she gets sentenced to life.

1913

Dombey and Son [3]

When I catch the English language,
its sound as shrill as a whistle,
I can see whole stacks of ledgers
and beneath them sits Oliver Twist.

Better to ask Charles Dickens
what London was like back then,
about Dombey's desk by the thick
and yellowish course of the Thames.

Rain and tears. That delicate head
belongs to The Dombey Son,
the only one who fails to get
the clerks' uproarious puns.

Collapsing chairs in the office.
Shillings and pence to count.
Like a hive of bees who've flown off,
all year, the figures swarm round.

But the sting of filthy barristers
works away as tobacco suffuses
the dark: like a bit of old bast,
the bankrupt dangles in a noose.

His enemies have laws on their side.
Nothing now can halt his losses.
Flinging her arms round his trouser-stripes,
his daughter breaks into sobs.

1913

Poisoned bread, not a drop in the air,
wounds that no one can treat:
Joseph, sold to the land of Pharaoh,
at the farthest boundary of grief.

In the starlight the Bedouin compose
wild epics on how they survived
the day's dangers, eyes now closed
up there on the horses they ride.

Out on the sand, a quiver was lost,
a horse-deal done – little
is needed to set the muse off,
so the mist of events will lift.

Even though all that will vanish,
if the song is true in the lungs,
there are things that remain: the expanse,
the stars and the voice that has sung.

1913

[Valkyries] 4

The violins call and the valkyries fly
as the opera lumbers to a close.
Footmen on marble stairs mark time,
clutching their ladies' and lords' fur-coats.

High in the gods, some fool claps on,
the final curtain good to descend.
Cabmen do jigs around their bonfire.
So-and-so's coach! Let's go. The End.

1914

Let's rhyme about Rome, that city of wonders
the cupola's victory founded and fortified,
and let the apostles' creed be our guide
as rainbows float in the drifting dust.

Twelve festival eves have always waited
up on the Aventine's heights for the emperor;
the strictly canonical moons will never
be fit to revise those calendar dates.

Above the Forum, the moon's huge shape
sprinkles brown cinders into the air
and across the valley. My head is bare:
cold is the Catholic's shaven pate.

1914

"Ice cream!" Sun. The airy biscuits.
A see-through tumbler filled with ice.
A chocolate world, where a daydream flies
into pink dawns and Alpine milkiness.

Look sweetly once you've tinkled the teaspoon.
In tiny pavilions, under dusty acacias,
accept and praise the bakers' graces,
fragile in intricate cups you'll consume…

The roaming ice-box, its lid embossed,
will be here soon – the barrel organ's friend.
And the street boy keeps his greedy attention
on that full coffer, its marvellous frost.

Gods couldn't say which one's in line:
cream diamonds or wafer plus filling? It glitters
in the sun, beneath that delicate splinter,
quick to vanish, the ice that's divine.

1914

Let the brief names of the flowering cities
fondle the ear with intelligibility;
no Rome lives on as the centuries pass
but humanity's place in the thick of the stars.

Emperors endeavour to wrest its command,
and the priests will approve all calls to arms.
Weep over them there, those altars and houses,
scorn them like sweepings if they live without it.

1914

from

Tristia

A Menagerie

Peace, that word we deleted
to begin an indignant age,
that lamp at the back of a cave,
the air in the Alps, now ether,
an ether we're neither willing
nor even able to breathe:
once more, the goatish reeds
of the shaggy pipes are singing.

While the lamb and the bullock
strayed over the over-fed fields,
and the friendship-loving eagles
perched on slumbering rocks,
an eagle was reared by the Teutons,
a lion was tamed by the British,
and there – well, how could you miss it? –
stood the crest of the Gallic rooster.

But now, the savage has mastered
old Heracles' sacred club,
and the blackened earth's dried up,
ungrateful as ground in the past.
So I'll take those sticks I've found
and kindle us all a fire.
Out with you into the soundless night,
you animal that I've roused!

We'll make a cage for this war,
for the rooster, lion, the gentle bear,
the eagle frowning into the air,
keep fur and feathers warm.
But I sing the wine of the Ages –
Italian spouts from a crack;
both Slavic and Germanic flax
quilt the Old Aryan cradle.

How can Italia muster the energy
to roll out the chariots of Rome?
That cackling livestock's wings have flown
up over its wicker fence.
Don't come here debt-collecting –
an eagle will bristle and anger:
neighbour, what if the rock in your hand
is cold and won't fit your sling?

Once these beasts are locked in cages,
the Volga's course will broaden,
the Rhine's current will brighten,
our noisy unease assuaged.
The wise will honour the stranger, as if
a demigod, quite unwilled,
and greet his arrival, dancing a wild
rite on the banks of great rivers.

1916

The night that can't be undone:
where you are, though, it's day.
I saw a black sun dawn
above Jerusalem's gates.

The yellow sun's more terrible –
a lullaby lulls in that light –
Jews in their shining temple
performed my mother's rites.

Without the hope of paradise,
without the holy masses,
in the bright temple the Israelites
chanted off a woman's ashes.

And every voice was a bell
as it sounded above my mother.
I woke inside a cradle,
and the light was that black sun's.

1916

Salamis, breath-taking island,
lay in view of the harbour at Athens,
severed by hands that were hostile.
The warlike Achaeans had gathered.

Now friends from distant isles
have come to fit out our ships,
but the British have never much prized
the honeyed soil that's Europe's.

Calling the European Hellenes,
protect Piraeus, the Acropolis!
Gifts from an island? Who needs
those ships' uninvited forest? [5]

1916

The Decembrist [6]

"Of this, the heathen senate is witness –
these deeds will never perish!"
He ruffled his gown. His pipe was lit.
Two friends went on with their chess.

He'd swapped his ambitions for felling timber
in the school of Siberian silence,
then the fancy pipe at his venomous lips,
but the world that listened was hostile.

Europe was weeping, clenched in a snare,
and the German oaks were stirring.
Black quadrigas reared in the air
atop triumphal about-turns.

Once, the blue punch would flame in our beakers
beside the roar of the samovar,
and the Nymph of the Rhine would softly speak,
that liberty-loving guitar.

"Voices alive continue to tremble
with talk of the sovereign citizen.
But what do the heroes want? Not heaven
gone blind, but work and persistence."

Colder and colder it gets by degrees,
and nobody catches your cry
that it's all muddled up. You sweetly repeat:
Russia, Lethe, Loreley.

1917

[*To Vera and Serge Sudeikin*] [7]

Our hostess had time to say a few words while the stream
of honey flowed on, so long and thick and golden –
"No, we're not bored here at all, in dreary Taurida [8]
where fate has brought us" – then glanced back over her shoulder.

Around us, a Bacchic ritual. As if it were dogs
and watchmen that ruled the earth, you walk and your eyes
find no one. The tranquil days roll on like kegs:
branches shelter the words you don't catch or reply to.

We took tea, and then went into the huge brown garden.
Eyelash-like, dark blinds were hiding the windows.
Past the white columns we walked and on to the vineyard,
the air a glaze poured over the slopes as they doze.

"It resembles a battle," I said, "in ancient times,
where the curly horsemen jostled in ornate formations:
here in stony Taurida we find Greek science
in these noble, rust-coloured rows, their golden acres."

The white room lies like a spinning wheel in silence.
It smells of vinegar, paint, fresh wine from the cellar.
Remember how long that Greek wife stitched her lines,
the one they all loved? And no, I don't mean Helen.

Where have you got to now, oh Golden Fleece?
The whole of the path was filled with the noise of the waves.
Abandoning ship, from the canvas-straining seas,
Odysseus made for home, full of time and space.

1917

[Meganom] [9]

The asphodels' [10] distant springtime
is still a transparent greyness,
and the sand's rustling continues
as the waves rage on, oh yes.
But like Persephone, my soul
has joined a light-footed round.
And the dead? Their empire holds
no shapely, sun-tanned hands.

Why then do we entrust
the urn's burden to a boat
across the water's amethyst
to feast it there with black roses?
Something draws my soul
out past the fog of Meganom;
the funeral done, a black sail
will round that cape for home.

How quickly the rainclouds cross
the ridge that lies unillumined,
and the flakes of those black roses
float in the moonlit wind.
We see the giant flag
of remembrance form a bird
of grief and death, and drag
on at the cypress stern.

The past is a paper fan
that gives a melancholy flutter.
Towards an amulet in sand,
hidden with a sombre shudder,
something draws my soul
out past the fog of Meganom –

the funeral done, a black sail
will round that cape for home.

1917

Tristia

I've studied the science of separation
at wakes where women wear their hair simply.
Oxen chewing, the mourners patient:
the watch's final hour in the city.
I keep the rites of the cockerel night,
as they raise the road's bitter burden,
and gaze out into that space, red-eyed,
where sobs and the muses' songs are heard.

But who can hear that word, *separation,*
and know just what goodbye we'll adopt,
what cockerels reveal in their exclamations
as fires burn inside the Acropolis?
Or on some kind of new life's brink,
while oxen chomp beneath tarpaulins –
why does the cockerel flutter its wings
as the *vita nova*'s proclaimed from the walls?

The shuttle warps, the spindle hums:
I love the common, humdrum threads.
Watch barefoot Delia, here she comes
towards us, like a swan's white feather,
aloft! Our life's a slender weft;
scanty, now, are the tongue's delights.
What happened once will happen afresh.
The instant's all we taste and recognize.

Well, so be it: a glassy manikin
lies on a pristine, earthenware plate,
resembling a squirrel's unfolded skin –
a girl bends over the wax and waits.
Predicting the underworld's not our task:
wax is for women, bronze is for men.

War's the one time our lots are cast,
prophecy their gift all the way to the end.

1918

As if we'd laid the sun in the ground,
we'll meet in Petersburg again,
the first occasion our lips pronounce
a sacred word that makes no sense.
In the black velvet of Soviet[11] nights,
in the velvet, global void, the song
in saintlike wives' familiar eyes
will sound, unfading flowers flower on.

The capital bends its back like a cat,
a patrol halts on a bridge, and all
that hurtles its way through the shadows
is an engine, with its cuckoo's call.
To pass this night I need no papers,
and I'm not frightened of sentries:
this Soviet night, my lips will pray
for a sacred word that makes no sense.

I hear a light, theatrical rustle
and catch the hint of a female sigh –
an enormous heap of unfading roses
lies in the hands of Cypris.[12]
Around a bonfire, we warm ourselves,
perhaps the centuries may proceed,
familiar hands of saintlike wives
will gather the ash in the tedium.

Somewhere, the dark, familiar pupils,
the dulcet choirs of Orpheus above,
and onto the ridges of seats, the playbills
fall from the galleries like doves. [13]
While no one notes the night sun, they'll sing,
those wives with shoulders aslope.

These are our candles for you to extinguish
as black velvet envelops the globe.

1920

I miss mosquitoes in winter,
buzzing our walls no more.
But you, my friend, you make me think
back to that light-headed straw.

Fashion does rings in the air
like a swallow, and dragonflies drone –
is that some basket snug round your hair
or a new kind of fluffed-up poem?

I won't go giving advice –
what good would persuasion be?
But still, the aroma of orange rind
lives on, and the taste of cream.

You think things through at random,
but you, you're none the worse.
I know your tender thoughts abandon
your mind and then disperse.

The spoon you're whisking a yolk with
has worked itself into a rage.
But though the yolk's all white and broken,
the spoon keeps whisking away.

Not a jot of all this is your fault.
Inside-out dresses, and grades –
what good are they? For you've been born
to squabble on the comedy stage.

You're one big song and tickle,
Italian roulade on a plate.
And now your slender, cherry-red lips
request a bunch of dry grapes.

No need to be clever – relax.
Your moments approach and pass.
A shadow falls from your knitted hat,
and it's that of a carnival mask.

1920

from

*Poems
1921–1925*

Concert at a Railway Station

Breathing is banned, and the night sky teems
with worms. Though stars are mute, there's music
over our heads that God has seen:
the station shivers with chorusing muses,
it's filled with fiddles in the midst of the steam;
torn by whistles once more, the air fuses.

A globe of glass. A park, enormous.
This world of iron's trance is deep.
A coach is moving off to the raucous
feast at a misty Elysian retreat.
A peacock squeals. The piano's victorious.
I'm late. And afraid. And asleep.

The violin chords have whirled and cried,
I enter the forest of glass, alone.
The first of the night choir's notes are wild;
in the rotting hotbeds, the roses' aroma.
My native shadow lay here for a night
beneath a glass sky, among teams of nomads.

Bathed in music and lather, it shakes
like a beggar, this world of iron that links
the glassy halls I lean back into.
Where are you off to? At the shadow's wake,
for one last time, our music sings.

1921

One night, as I washed in the yard,
the sky was bright with milled stars,
and a beam shone like salt on the axe.
The barrel was brimming with ice.

The gates were bolted and locked,
and believe me, the earth is strict.
You won't find a line that's cleaner
than the truth there is in fresh linen.

A star dissolved like salt in the barrel,
and the ice-cold water blackened.
A cleaner death and saltier trouble,
the earth more truthful and terrible.

1921

Light Rain in Moscow

The skinflint rain in summer
doles out the chill the sky stores.
This bit's ours. That's for the clumps
of trees, and this for the cherry stalls.

The boiling starts in the dusk
with the light fussing of teapots,
an anthill filling the sky
is feasting upon dark shoots;

and a vineyard of glistening droplets
begins to sway in the grass,
revealing a coldness potted
in Moscow, whose shape is a palm's.

1922

Century

Brute of an age, who could look
into your tapering eyes?
And if they used their blood, glue back
two centuries' severed spine?
Blood the Builder scourges and flows
from the throat of things terrestrial.
And on the era's threshold, those
who scrounge at our backs will tremble.

While life still haunts it, all creation
hauls around its vertebrae,
and every swelling wave will play
with the spine that we can't see.
The new-born age on earth resembles
an infant's cartilage. Life
is a braying lamb yanked off again
by the top of the head to the knife.

To free the century from confinement,
so the new world might appear,
we'll have to snatch a flute to bind
the tunes of our tangled years.
This is the century which will heave
human anguish like a wave,
and in the grass the viper breathes
by the century's golden ratio.

Now the tips of the buds extend,
crops' green shoots will splash.
Hey, my terrible, splendid century,
your spine's completely smashed.
Cruel and weak, with a senseless smile,
you turn your eyes towards us,
a beast that we'd have once called lithe,
now on the trail of its claws.

[Blood the Builder scourges and flows
from the throat of terrestrial things.
A feverish fish splashes the coast,
its warm tissue of shingle.
And streaming from the birds' high gauze –
the moist masses in the blue –
sheer indifference pours and pours
straight onto your fatal wound.][14]

1922

The Man who Finds the Horseshoe

(A Pindaric fragment)

Let's gaze at the forest and say:
This is a boat forest, a mast forest,
with its rosy fir-trees
free of their furry burdens up to their tops.
They'll give a good creak in a storm,
these solitary pines,
in that furious, treeless air:
fixed on a reeling deck, their plumbline
                    withstands the salty heel of the wind.
In the limitless thirst of the ocean,
the navigator
drags his fragile geometrical instrument across the wet ruts
and checks the rugged sea surface
against the gravity, earth's embrace.

But as we inhale the tar and the scent of its tears
that have oozed their way through the skin of the ship,
and admire the planks
riveted up in seamless bulkheads –
not as Bethlehem's peaceful carpenter might have,
but citing the father of voyages, the mariner's mate –
we'll say:
They too once stood on the earth,
earth as comfortable as a donkey's backbone,
their tops on a glamorous ridge
forgetting their roots.
Noisy in the downpour of fresh water,
they'd turn to the sky and ask it in vain
to barter its precious load
for a pinch of salt.

How shall we start?
Everything creaks and rocks.

The air trembles with similes.
No word's better than the next.
The earth hoots with metaphor,
and light chariots –
with their gaudy harness of bird flocks dense with effort –
splinter into pieces,
competing with hippodromes' snorting favourites.

Thrice-blessed be those who swear a name into song;
a song lives longer
adorned with a name,
as if friends had bound your head with a band to honour that song
and save you from forgetfulness, that stupefying smell
like a man's proximity,
a fierce animal's fur
or simply the scent of savory crushed in the hand.

Life is a fish that swims the air's dark water,
forcing apart that dense,
warm, elastic sphere with its fins –
a crystal where wheels rattle and horses shy,
Neaera's[15] damp black earth that pitchforks, tridents, hoes and shares
plough up each night.
The air as stiffly kneaded as earth:
impossible to leave and difficult to enter.

A rustle runs through the woods like a green *lapta*[16] club.
Kids play jacks with the spines of dead animals.
Our era's fragile counting of summers nears its end.
My thanks for the things that have been:
I lost my way, the plot and the score.
The era would chime like a golden ball
held up by no one, cored and cast.
When touched, it would answer "yea" or "nay",
like a child's reply:
"An apple for you" or "No apple for you" –
the face a faithful mould of the voice pronouncing these words.

The sound resounds, though its origin's gone.
The stallion lies in the dust and a lather of sweat, snorting.
But the steep crook of its neck
preserves the memory of galloping legs flung about –
not four in number
but as many as the stones on the road,
refreshed in four changes,
the number of times that ambler panting with heat repulses the earth.

So
the man who finds the horseshoe
blows off the dust
and rubs the iron with wool till it shines;
then
he hangs it above his doorway
where it can rest
and never chip sparks from the flint again.
Human lips with no more to say
retain the shape of the last word said,
a sensation of weight stays in the hand
though half the jug's splashed out by the time it's home.

I did not say what I said, these things
are dug from the ground like grains of petrified wheat.
Some
    put lions on coins,
others
    put heads.
These biscuits of copper, of gold and bronze
hide in the earth in their various shapes
and with the same honour.
The age has left the print of its teeth as it tries to gnaw through them.
Time is clipping my coin,
and even for me, my value's fallen.

1923

The Ode on Slate [17]

The mighty juncture of star upon star,
the flint path formed from ancient song,
language of flint and language of air –
flint join water, horseshoe join ring –
sketched on a slate, a milky paleness.
That is no exercise set for the spheres
across the clouds, their yielding shale,
but the blinking, dreaming sheep's delirium.

We sleep on our feet in the crowded dark,
under a warming sheep's wool hat.
Like a chain or a warbler, as if it were talking,
into its shoring, the spring babbles back.
With milky strokes from leaden wands,
here, it's fear and the fault that write;
here, it's the water cascading onwards
whose pupils' notebooks are almost ripe.

The goats have got their precipitous towns,
the flint its mighty strata, still
there are higher ridges and ridges around us,
hamlets and chapels in sheep-ruled hills.
Water their tutor, time their miller,
down to preach each week's the plumbline.
The air's transparent forest long filled
with the bursting moisture of all that's done.

The gaudy day's a lifeless hornet
swept from its comb in the hive, disgraced;
night's a black kite whose claws are drawn
and hold bright chalk to nourish the slate.
The iconoclastic slabs to hand,
we'd wipe away our day's impressions,
shaking their near-translucent phantoms
from our arms as if they were fledglings!

The grapes have ripened. The fruit has swelled.
The day has raged as days will rage.
The game of knucklebones looks so delicate,
sheepdogs growl and gleam at midday;
and like the icy summits' waste –
green patterns reversed, revealing seams –
resembling a whelp with a tail to chase,
the hungering water whirls and streams

and crawls towards me, miming a spider,
across the moon-wet joins; agape
up there on the gaping, starry heights
I start to hear that squealing slate.
[Are those your voices wanting to teach us,
memory, chipping at night in its quarries,
ripping the slate from the avian beaks
to scatter its fragments across the forest?

Only the voice is able to state
what used to be there, what scratched and fought.
We'll lead the unfeeling slate to the place
the voice will point our steps towards.][18]
Burning chalk I take to harden
the moment in writing, I'll quarry the night,
swap sound for the arrow's song and bargain
harmony away for the bustard's spite.[19]

Who am I then? I'm not straight up,
no honest roofer, shipwright, mason.[20]
I double-deal, my soul is double,
mate of the nights and scout for the days.
Blessed are those who'll say the flint
was always the flowing water's disciple,
who've stood on solid soil and hitched
a sandal strap to the sole of the hill.

The summer has left a diary of scratches
on slate, at which I study away,
at the air and the flint's recorded language,
strata of darkness, luminous layer;
into the path that flint has formed
from ancient song, I want my fingers
to thrust and then to seal that sore:
flint join water, horseshoe join ring.

1923, [1937]

Through the gypsy camp of the darkened street, I'll rush
after a cherry branch bouncing away in a carriage,
its bonnet of snow and endless din like a millstone.

All I recall's how the chestnut locks misfired
and their smoky bitterness – better to say, ant acid.
Their amber dryness lingers here on my lips.

Even the air looks hazel in minutes like these,
the rings encircling the pupils wear light edges;
I know that skin, every inch as pink as an apple…

But on that cab, the sledge-runners kept on squeaking,
thornlike stars looked in through the bast, the hooves
were striking an icy keyboard, letters typed out.

Even the light's full of starlike, thorny lies;
life bobs across that theatrical bonnet's froth.
No one catches my words: "From the dark street's camp…"

1925

from

New Verses

What dreadful spot are we headed for now,
comrade blessed with a supersized mouth?

Oh, our tobacco's crumbling to bits,
my nutcracking friend, quite out of your wits!

Well, we could whistle though life, like starlings,
or sweeten its taste with a peck of nut tart.

That's one more plan I doubt will hit.

October 1930

Armenia

> *To the people here, labour's a bull,*
> *terrible and with six wings.*
> *The roses' veins are looking full,*
> *roses that bloom before winter.* [21]

1

Rocking Hafiz's rose,
wild cub and nestling's nurse,
you breathe from the eight-flanked shoulders
of the peasants' bullish church.

Daubed in ochre gone hoarse,
you lie beyond that range.
And the print that adheres to the saucer
is the only thing that remains.

2

My vision had vanished, and my poor ears had gone deaf,
the gruff red ochres the only tones I'd got left.

For some reason I'd dreamt of Armenian mornings, and planned
to examine the blue tit's habits in Yerevan,

how the baker stoops in his game of blind man's buff
to peel the loaves' moist hides from the walls of the oven.

Yerevan, Yerevan, did a bird sketch out your lines?
Who coloured you in like a child with crayons, a lion?

Yerevan, Yerevan, you roasted nut of a city,
I love your big-mouthed streets' Babylonian twists.

I thumbed through a muddled-up life, like a mullah his Koran.
I froze my time, did nobody's veins any harm.

Yerevan, Yerevan, there's nothing at all I crave
or need any more. I'll leave you your icy grapes.

3

You wanted pigments to draw with
and so, from out of its case,
the Lion of Lines would paw
and snatch a half-dozen crayons.

Land of paint-merchants' hearths
and potters working dead plains,
you endured the red-bearded Sardars
in the middle of stone and clay.

Far from the anchors and tridents,
some love life and its pleasures
where the rocks rested and dried,
others love punishment measures.

Plain as a child's drawing,
and hastening no tide through
my blood, the women who walk here
distribute a lion's beauty.

Your youthful graves, your ominous
language warm my thoughts;
your letters are blacksmith's tongs,
each word is a clamp from the forge…

4

With your mouth muffled up like a wet rose
and the eight-sided honeycombs you held,

in the early mornings, you'd gulp back your tears
as you waited on the outskirts of the world.

You showed your back, in shame and grief,
to the bearded cities of the East.
Now you lie on the paint-merchant's bed
in the death mask they're easing off.

5

Wrap a shawl round your hand and sink it
into the briar's thick and celluloid thorns.
Be bold about it. Thrust on till it crunches!
We'll have that rose out, without shears.
But careful it doesn't all crumble straight off:
litter of roses – lattice – a Solomon's petal.
Wild and no good for sherbet,
it won't yield scent or oil.

6

Domain of bellowing stones,
Armenia, Armenia;
calling the hoarse-mouthed peaks to weapons,
Armenia, Armenia.
Winging your way towards Asia's trumpets of silver,
Armenia, Armenia;
scattering Persian coins, you dole the sun out at will,
Armenia, Armenia.

7

No, not ruins but timber robbed from the huge compass forest,
the anchoring stumps of the felled oaks of a fable-and-beast Christianity –
the rolls of stone cloth that top the columns, ransacked from pagan traders,
and grapes the size of pigeon-eggs, rams with flourishing horns,
and ruffled eagles with owl's wings, that Byzantium left undefiled.

8

The rose is cold in the snow:
    three yards of it on Sevan Island…
    A mountain fisherman drags his patterned, sky-blue sledge out,
    the whiskered mouths of the well-fed trout
    perform police duties
    over the lime of the lakebed.

But in Yerevan and Echmiadzin
    the massive mountain's gulped up the air,
    you'd need an ocarina's[22] high notes to charm it,
    a dudka[23] to tame it,
            for the snow to thaw in your mouth.

Snow, snow, snow on rice paper,
    the mountain floats to my lips.
    I'm cold and glad.

9

A squalid hamlet, but hear the splendid
hairlike music of water!
A sound or a thread? Or is it a warning?
Get thee gone – we're nearing the end!

And in that maze of moist voices
the stifling mist fills with insect sounds,
as if some nymph's come round to visit
the watchmaker who lives underground.

10

The hooves of the stumbling farmhorse
clatter as she tries to mount
the State's bald plinth
whose purple granite resounds.

Behind her, barely pausing for breath,
come the Kurdish knotters of cheese,
who've brokered peace between God and the Devil
and render one half unto each.

11

Azure and clay, the clay and azure.
What more could you want? So come on and squint,
like a short-sighted shah at a turquoise ring,
at the book of resonant clay, the earth
become book, the festering book, a clay road
we make our ordeal, as if it were music and word.

12

So this is the last time I'll see you,
myopic Armenian sky,
my final glance as I blink
at Ararat, its roadside tent,
my final time in the library
of perfect earth that potters wrote with,
where I opened the hollow volume
the first humans took as their tutor.

16 October – 5 November 1930

[Leningrad] 24

It knows me, this city I'd walk till I cried,
that I knew to my veins and swollen glands as a child.

You're back in your city now: quicker and quicker,
swallow its fish oil from the lamps by the river.

Make out December's daylight fast,
where a yolk is mixed into the sinister tar.

Petersburg, I don't want to die just yet:
out with those phone numbers of mine you've kept!

Petersburg, every address in my head
will help me track down a voice from the dead.

I live on a black staircase, where the doorbell
torn from the flesh batters my temples.

All night, I wait for our friends to call,
as I move the chains, like shackles, on the door.

December 1930

Like the bulk of a nation starting
to make the mantle sweat,
the dust-encrusted armada
of a herd, with its many strata,
sails right into my head:

the heifers – their tender sides –
the tearaway bullocks, the ships
of the buffalo loom into sight,
female and male, and behind them,
the bulls tramp up like bishops.

June 1931

Lamarck

There once was a timid old man, as shy
as a lad, a clumsy patriarch...
Just who was nature's champion? Why,
that fiery fencer, Lamarck.

If life's no more than a blot in a lab,
in the brief, escheated[25] sunshine,
then on that Lamarckian rolling ladder
the final rung will be mine.

I'll swish down past the lizards and snakes,
descend to the cirripeds and annelids
along shifting gangways, into their nooks,
I'll shrink to a proteus, vanish.

I'll deny my veins' warm blood and then
wear corneous cloaks, overgrown
with suckers, my brain instruct a tendril
to pierce the ocean foam.

We went through the eyes of the insect classes,
shot-glasses full to the brim.
Vision's a myth – you've seen your last –
nature's in fissures, he put in.

Enough of fine sounds, all your sense
of Mozart's for nothing, he said.
The breakdown is stronger than all our strength;
here comes the spider's deaf tread.

And now that nature's retreated a pace,
we're the stage it no longer needs,
the *medulla oblongata*[26] placed
like a sword inside a dark sheath.

Its memory faltering, nature has lagged
in letting its drawbridge descend
for those whose laughter's adept at adapting,
whose graves are green and breath red.

7 – 9 May 1932

Impressionism

The artist portrays the deep faint
of the lilac for us, as he dabs
his canvas, placing the scab-like,
resounding footsteps of paint.

He adds thick oil, understands
how the summer his hands have been baking
is rewarmed in violet brains: once taken
by the stifling heat, it expands.

And the shadow shades into violet!
A whistle or whip's a snuffed match.
Your analysis: "Chefs in a kitchen,
putting plump pigeons to the knife."

There's a swing here, for those in the know,
and veils not quite fine-grained;
now, in the sunlight's disintegration,
it's the bumble bee running this show.

23 May 1932

To the German Language

For B.C. Kuzin [27]

> [Freund! Versäume nicht zu leben:
> Denn die Jahre fliehn,
> Und es wird der Saft der Reben
> Uns nicht lange glühn! [28]
>   —Ewald Christian Kleist [29]]

My way to ruin and rant at myself,
like a midnight moth hellbent on a flame,
there's a need to escape our speech I've felt,
the lifelong terms by which I'm constrained.

No false praise can squeeze between us,
we're not two-faced but point-blank friends.
Let's learn some respect and to say what we mean
from a family over our Western fence.

Think of the storms – fantastic for poems!
Permit me, my art, to point out the hilt
that fine *Kapitän* would entangle in roses,
Ceres[30] the name encrusting his lips.

Frankfurt echoed with fathers' yawns,
there'd been no news of Goethe just yet.
Hymns were composed, you saw how horses
pranced and leapt on the spot like letters.

Tell me in which Valhalla we'd stop
and sit, my friends, to crack those nuts.
What kind of freedom was it you offered?
Which of my landmarks did you construct?

Out of an almanac's pages, straight
down the steps to your tomb you ran,
out of that first-class news, unafraid,
as if just fetching Mosel by the tankard.

A stranger's language will be my skin.
Still too timid to be born as yet,
I was a letter, a stitch in a vineyard,
I was the book of which you'd dreamt.

I had no face or faith till friendship
roused my sleeping soul like a shot.
Give me the fate of Pylades,[31] or rip
my useless tongue out, *Nachtigallgott.*

Nightingale god, they'll still recruit me
for seven-year slaughters, new rounds of pestilence.
Sounds taper off and words hiss mutiny,
but you're alive, and you and I are at rest.

8 – 12 August 1932

We live, but feel no land at our feet,
nor ten steps off any whisper of speech.
Where half a conversation finds enough lips,
it's the Kremlin-Climber our thoughts are with.
His weighty fingers as greasy as worms,
true as a dumbbell tumble his words.
His laughing moustache is cockroach-huge,
there's a gleam from the tops of his boots.

Around him, the rabble of slim-necked princes,
half-human officials, their labours his playthings.
One whines like a cat, one whistles or snivels
as he blabs and jabs at them; the gifts he gives,
decree by decree, he pounds like iron
into groin, into crown, into brow, into eye –
lemons,[32] no matter what capital offence,
and it's broad, that Ossetian chest.

November 1933

from

The Voronezh Notebooks

From the *First Notebook*

I live in key kitchen gardens
where Ivan the Steward[33] could've strolled.
The wind volunteers in the mills;
a path of logs absconds ever farther.

Numb in the lights as tiny as beads,
the Black Earth night on the rim of the steppe.
Right through the wall, a stranger stomps
his bad mood off, in his Russian boots:

I don't sleep well to the sound of our host.
That rented floorboard is all crooked,
a coffin's plank in this vessel's deck,
where death and the kiosk are all that's close.

April 1935

Hey there, Earphones, Earphones you snitch!
I'll keep these Voronezh nights in mind.
The voice's vin d'Ay[34] continues to fizz,
at twelve I can hear the Red Square chimes.

What's the Metro like? Well keep that to yourself,
but don't ask how far the spring buds have got.
Kremlin clock, up there, your bells
are the speech of the cosmos shrunk to a full stop.

April 1935

Voronezh, Crow-Town, permit me to go:
you run me to the verge, but preserve my knowledge,
you rent me a niche as I veer near the edge,
random Voronezh, ruining town of crows.

Give me back and let me go,
you'll let me fall or else you'll fumble,
you'll give me up or drop me, dump me,
town whose name's a knife and crow.[35]

April 1935

What street are we on?
Mandelstam Street.
Damned if I know what that name means.
Try to unscrew it it still sounds wrong,
all twisted and not very clean.

The way he did things could have been straighter,
his self-control a little greater,
and that's why this street –
just a gutter really –
down by the rails
has a sign on which stands
the name of that Mandelstam.

April 1935

Black Earth

Hallowed and black, it's all under nurture,
all horse's shoulder, all air and care,
all of it crumbling, one huge choir –
my land and liberty's[36] clods of damp turf.

The black turns blue as they plough at dawn;
foundation of unarmed labour, a thousand
rumoured hills have succumbed to the foreshare:
the district doesn't fit with the land that surrounds us.

It's a sledgehammer though, a *faux pas*, this earth:
it allows no appeals as you thud down your head,
with its mouldering flutes, puts your ears on alert,
will till them for spring with its morning clarinet.

How well that rich layer lies on the plough,
how well the steppe sits on a crankshaft in April!
So I greet you, black earth: be round-eyed and stout…
The black-tongued silence that's found in labour.

April 1935

You took away my seas, the run and the running jump,
and brought my toes to rest on the earth now violated,
achieving what? Yes, brilliant the way you settled up:
lips that won't stop twitching can't be amputated.

May 1935

[The River Kama]

[1]

Oh, on the Kama, black out when you see
how the towns are down on their oaken knees.

Dressed in webs, beards brushing together,
the burning fir-grove runs into the water.

On a hundred and four oars, upstream, downstream,
the water flows on to Kazan and Cherdyn.

With the curtain pulled, I was floating by,
with the curtain pulled and my head in that fire.

For five nights my wife didn't sleep at my side,
five nights until she and her escorts arrived.

[2]

[Oh, on the Kama, black out when you see
how the towns are down on their oaken knees.

Dressed in webs, beards brushing together,
the burning fir-grove runs into the water.

On a hundred and four oars, upstream, downstream,
the water flows on to Kazan and Cherdyn.

Mighty as peasants, and parched as low woods,
a shoal of logs would scatter like bullets.

The Ob splashes rafts. From the Tobol come cries.[37]
The riverside milestones rise to the heights.][38]

[3]

The coniferous East receded, I saw
the Kama's full waters bear down on a buoy.

I wanted to burn myself gaps on those slopes,
but barely had time to season the groves.

I wanted new roots, if you follow my sense,
in the Urals' longevity, among its settlements.

I wanted this glassy, delirious surface
in my overcoat's flaps, to hold and preserve it.

April – May 1935

We're brimming with life, and that's capital: [39]
through Soviet cities, Chinese
blouses and dresses continue to amble,
patterned with butterflies and leaves.

The acrid clippers give Grade Ones,
collecting their chestnut bribes;
it falls judiciously, the hair now on
clean aprons, in thickening stripes.

Swallows and swifts delight us,
no comet's plague yet spreads.
The purple inks continue to write
with stars and tails, to make sense.

25 May 1935

The full-weight ingots of Roman nights,
the female form young Goethe spotted –
hold me at fault, but leave me in pocket:
many are the depths in an outlaw's life.

June 1935

St. Isaac's freezes to each dead eyelash;
on the aristocratic blue streets,
like wolf-tails – strangers' logs in the ash,
an organ grinder's death, bear fleece.

Ungripping that pack from its leash, the whipper-in
whips out the fire, and it starts to sprawl.
The furnished globe of the earth is spinning,
and the face-pulling mirror plays the know-all.

The staircase landing's all squabbles and mist,
breathing, breathing and song.
Schubert's talisman's cold and stiff
beneath the fur coat. Keep on, keep on…

3 June 1935

From the *Second Notebook*

The Birth of the Smile

When the face of a child first forks
into smiles of pleasure and passion,
the tips of those smiles aren't telling us jokes
but sailing out onto a chaotic expanse.

Things are just fine: amid that fame,
the lips are at play, already stitching
away at the seams that form the rainbow
the child will ply for constant cognition.

The mother continent crawls from the ocean:
that Atlantean moment buffets the eyes,
the mouth a cochlea, an inrush approaching,
and we gently playact our praise and surprise.

8 December 1936 – 17 January 1937

I marvel at the kids and snow,⁴⁰
and at the light some more –
no faithful servant but a road,
this smile that no one's forged.

December 1936 – 1938 (?)

Goldfinch friend, when I tilt my head
we see the world like twins.
But is the spiky sky – think seed –
as cruel in your pupil this winter?

Yellow and black, your tail like a boat,
below your beak you blush.
Did you know that you're so goldfinch,
the goldfinch kind this much?

Black and yellow, red and white.
The air gone into that crown!
He keeps his eyes peeled either side –
then stops – and off he's flown.

9 – 27 December 1936

Today is kind of yellow-gobbed,
I can't say why. The gates
to the sea pierce anchors and fog
to fix me with their gaze.

Silent warships pace and pace,
the water loses its dyes,
and each canal's a pencil case,
blacker beneath the ice.

9 – 28 December 1936

Inside the mountain, the idol sits idly
in enormous, cautious, contented halls.
Necklaces drip down his neck like oil
to guard his dreams, their high and low tides.

An Indian rainbow his daily meal,
back then as a boy, the peacock his playmate,
he drank his milk out of rose-tinged clay,
and they did not skimp on the cochineal.[41]

His bundle of bones remains there, drowsy,
his shoulders, elbows and hands have assumed
the flesh. He smiles with that wisest of mouths,
thinks in bones and observes from his brow,
straining to remember his face, once human.

10 – 26 December 1936

[Core of an ocean, this region [42]
floats on the top of dark waters
with buckets of thunder and heavens
of bread: these lands are no lord's.
I like their sharpened outline
as Africa's shape appears –
lights on! Now look at the countless
holes that bemoon the veneer: [43]
Anna, Rossosh, Gremyache[44] – over
and over I say their names;
white as eiders, the snows
you'll see through the glass from a train.

With a mouthful of air I wandered
about these fields, the State's.
Into my eyes, the sunflowers shone,
the farm's harsh suns, rotating.
In the dark we pulled into Tambov,
sleeve of a town, ablaze with snow.
I saw the Tsna, an ordinary river,
its utterly white white cloak.
My mind will hold on forever
to this labouring land I know,
and I will always remember
that district official, the sparrow.

Where the hell am I? What's wrong?
The steppe is bare without winter.
Koltsov's[45] stepmum? Come on,
it's the Motherland of the goldfinch!
Only the mute town surveyed
when the ground's crusted with ice,
only the kettle talking away
to itself on the steppe at night.

Amid the air's thickness,
the messages trains exchange,
sounding their long-winded whistles
that drawl away in Ukrainian.]

23 – 27 December 1936

The goldfinch goes into shudders
in its airy muffin, all cardiovital,
professor in its fine black cap, then spite
shakes pepper on its gown all of a sudden.

The cage's one hundred knitting needles
and the slat accuse it, the perch concurs.
And inside-out is all the earth:
a Salamanca[46] of trees indeed
for wise, disobedient birds.

December 1936

I feel the winter begin,
a belated gift. I love
its onset, love that swing
no one will quite believe.

A season pretty with fright,
the start of brutal business –
faced with a vista without forest,
even the raven grows timid.

But strongest of all are the pale
blue, temple-like bulges
of rounded ice, unstable
in the streams' unruly lullaby.

29 – 30 December 1936

It isn't cheap, this yeast:
the noise and tears and toil
are the planet's rhythmic rain
as disaster starts to boil.
What ore could help regain
the sounds our ears have lost?

When nothing's left, the mind
will first begin to sense
blind ruts the water fills,
whose copper lakes you follow,
unkind, unknown to yourself,
both blind man and his guide.

12 – 18 January 1937

January. Where can I go to vanish?
The open city⁴⁷ clings like a psychotic.
I could low as I pass each bolt and clamp,
have the doors got me drunk or what?

The yelping lanes take the form of tights,
the convoluted streets are storerooms
where youthful hoodlums hurriedly hide,
then leap like knights out of corners.

Into the warty gloom, its pit,
I stumble to the pump and find it frozen.
I feed on the blackdamp⁴⁸, skid
and scatter the feverish crows.

And into the planks of that iced-up box
I sigh and call, the crows now airborne:
"Talk to me! Readers, advisers, doctors,
these steps have turned into thorns."

1 February 1937

From the *Third Notebook*

Verses on the Unknown Soldier [49]

[1]

May this air be our witness,
his long-range heart back us up:
the dugouts are bustling, omnivorous,
their windowless ocean a substance.

These stars are total snitches!
Watching how witness and judge
are judged is none of their business,
nor this windowless ocean of substance.

Rain, the sullen sower, thinks back
(its manna of names unetched)
to how the forest of crosses marks
that sea and forms up in a wedge.

People weak from the cold
will kill, shiver and starve;
we billet the unknown soldier
down there in his famous grave.

Swallow who's lost the power to fly,
I've neither wings nor rudder,
but teach me a way I might
outwit that airy sepulchre.

Lieutenant Lermontov[50] has dispatched
me here with his dour reports
on how the grave straightens the slouch
and its air pocket pulls you off course.

[2]

Like a vineyard as it stirs,
they menace us, these worlds.
Spotted with grease all golden,
expanding constellations' tents
dangle the cities they've stolen,
the golden slanders and words not meant,
each berry, ah, its poisonous coldness…[51]

[2a]

[And through the ether, the decimally specified
light of velocities' fine-milled beam
begins to count, it's visible, bright
with pain, its zeroes a timber-filled stream.

Across the field of all fields there flies
a new field, formed like a crane's three corners.
The news is flying, dusty with light,
and yesterday's battle begets a new dawn.

Dusty with light, the news is flying:
I'm new. No, I'm not Waterloo.
Neither the Battle of Nations, nor Leipzig.
Let the world light up from whatever I do.]

[3]

A blood-soaked Arabian mess,
the light of velocities ground to a shaft.
There on my retina it rests,
the soles of its feet aslant.

Millions murdered on the cheap
have trodden their path in the void.
I wish them well and a good night's sleep
on behalf of the ramparts of soil.

Trench sky that takes no bribes,
manufactured, wholesale death
is your monopoly. I leave your lines,
and my lips drift in the darkness.

With an odour of smoke, sullen and pock-marked,
the spirit of the splintered graves
passes the screes, craters and ramparts
where it slowed and settled its haze.

[4]

How well the infantry die,
and the night choir sings over the top
of Švejk[52] and his snubby smile,
the avian lance of Don Quixote,
and the shins of the jousting poultry.
A cripple befriends another man,
and they won't go short of a job:
with their wooden crutches, a clan
clatters along the fence of the Age –
hey there, my global comrades!

[5]

Is that why the skull has to grow
into the forehead, right across it?
So soldiers can't help but overflow
into the eyes' precious sockets?
The size of the skull increases
as life commands it to grow
until it becomes a conscious cupola
that its own neat stitching teases.
The land of its lands, the cup of its cups,
a bonnet whose seam the stars have sown,
Shakespeare's father, its thoughts foam,
fortune's cap, it dreams itself up…

[6]

These aspens are clear, the maples precise,
their light whirls home with a crimson tinge
and overstocks the double skies
that seem to faint as the fire dims.

It's only excess with which we're allied.
No trap doors but fathoms before us:
the fight for a ration of air is a fight
unlike all other glories.

My half-dazed life has overstocked
the part of my mind that's aware.
Is this me, with no choice but to drink the broth
and consume my own head under fire?

These spells in the emptiness, why
did they bother to string them together
if the stars that left all white
hurtle home a little redder?

What's next for us now and hereafter, night
that the stars in their camp call stepmother?

[7]

Blood tautens the aortas.
The ranks vibrate with a whisper:
Born in eighteen ninety-four…
Born in eighteen ninety-six…
In the tight-packed lines of that horde,
with the tattered year I was born
gripped in my peasant's fist,
I whisper with blood-drained lips,
as I stand with the rest of my herd:
Born on the night that slipped

*from the second to the third
of January, the year uncertain,
some eighteen nineties' treachery…
Around me, the fire of the centuries.*

2 March 1937 – 1938

[Reims – Laon] [53]

I saw a lake stood sheer on its side
where fish wheeled round a severed rose,
building themselves their freshwater homes,
the boat where the fox and lion fight,

three baying doors where plagues would gaze,
the arches arch-enemies of unrevealed arches.
The spires on the cliff suspired with a start.
A gazelle leapt the arches' violet spaces.

True sandstone's risen, plied with moisture.
In this city built by crickets in guilds,
the ocean climbs from the stream and flings
beakers of water at clouds, a bad boy.

4 March 1937

So that the sandstone, mate of the wind[54]
and raindrops, would keep them safe,
the kings would scribble out bottles within
more bottles, and the egret's shape.

The sovereign shame of the Egyptians
put on the skins of the very best dogs,
and beneath the trivial pyramids' tips,
it assigned the dead their bits and bobs.

Hero of mine, you were something else,
an incorrigible, comforting balladeer;
we can hear that gnashing of teeth you left us,
plaintiff for ash that leaves behind fear.

You knitted twin testaments out of that tangle
of goods whose willpower was nil,
churred your farewells and then gave back
a world as profound as a skull.

He lived next door to the Gothic, misbehaved,
spitting on laws that spiders had spun,
that cheeky schoolboy and thieving angel,
the incomparable Monsieur Villon,

burglar to the celestial clergy.
It's no disgrace to sit at his side,
and the skylarks will still be chirping
when the end of the world's in sight.

18 March 1937

I raise these leaves to my lips,
greenery glued into an oath,
this perjurous earth that bore snowdrops,
mother of the maples and oaks.

See me grow strong and go blind
in my homage to humble roots;
my eyes find this park too fine
as the rumbling passes through.

Like beads of mercury, frogs
are linking their voices together;
branches form from twigs,
a milky figment from cold breath.

30 April 1937

[Verses to Natasha Shtempel] [55]

I

Crossing bare earth, she can't help tilting:
that walk of hers is all sweetly lop-sided.
She starts to outstrip by just a little
her nimble friend with a youthful admirer.
Drawing her onwards, a kind of liberty:
cramped, but a defect that's inspiring.
And maybe you'll find a clear theory
among her steps, intent on lingering,
the hunch that the weather this springtime
might be an Eve, our sepulchre sighted,
and all this will keep on beginning.

II

There are women for whom the earth's damp surface
is home, each step resounds with mourning.
Walking with the risen and being there early
to welcome the dead is still their calling.
It's a crime to ask these women for caresses:
no one can leave them. Today they're an angel,
tomorrow a worm in the earth's recesses,
and one day later no more than a contour.
The past is a stair no longer accessible.
The sky is entire. The flowers are immortal.
And the future's no more than a promise.

4 May 1937

Children's Poetry

Balloons

The babbling balloons were puffed-up and proud,
they dangled on string like a multi-coloured cloud
and floated and fussed and bumped into each other,
each of them clobbering its babier brother.

"Oh woe is Me That Is Green, from that bighead,
that terrible bully, the Balloon That Is Red.
I'm only a stray. I'm a total goon.
I'm really a dimwit, a silly balloon."

"Well, my string's as thin
as a cobweb's thread.
You won't find a wrinkle,
no not a single
one on the skin
of my airy head."

A wheezing barrel organ
peered up and saw them.
"Let's join the crowd
and follow that cloud.
They'll cheer up as soon
as I turn out a tune."

"Oh," said the willow,
"balloons are fun!
And they don't weigh a ton!
Let 'em all blow!"
Our puffed-up friends
fluffed up like hens…

Behind the stalls
they were short of change
but not of birdcalls

from the cages they'd arranged.
And here comes Bighead
poking his nose
into everything spread out
along those rows.

"Oh balloons of blue,
tied with white string,
I'll sell you off too,
my till will go ping!"

A purple one said:
"I'm not a biscuit!
A balloon am I!
If you think I won't fly
off with my thread,
go on, risk it!"

Oh friends who are airy!
Every canary
was chirping its song,
when a lad came along
who'd just had to pay
for a fine little whistle.
He was munching biscuits
and giving some away.
He started to count
that quarrelsome flock
knocking about,
all chock-a-block
on its tempting thread…
And he too had got
an enormous head!

They puffed and puckered, all those balloons,
purple red blue, as ripe as prunes.
"Please don't leave us here in this muddle!
Watch us move, we're special: we waddle!"

One of them would float
as proud as a flame,
one played the game
of the peacock's coat.
But here was that goon,
the stray green balloon.

"That green one's my thing,
so give me the string.
Hey Slow-Brain, don't trail
on the floor like a snail!
Fly off in the breeze
wherever you please!"

Balloons are fun!
And they don't weigh a ton!
Our puffed-up friends
fluffed up like hens…
And here comes Bighead
poking his nose
into everything spread out
along those rows.

1926

Ants

Don't go touching ants, I say.
Ten thousand of them, wielding goods,
have all been walking for three days,
jostling through the silent woods.

A super porter is our ant,
an absolutely total hunk.
Shiny, black, it doesn't pant
while struggling under its family trunk.

Like railway stations, huge and lavish,
those anthills dot the forest floor…
The ants will carry in their baggage
through door and hall and corridor!

The strongest and staunchest of them all
has now arrived – not a minute late –
at the great building, with its storeys
piled up there, all forty-eight.

Published 1924

The Egg

Once an egg ticked off a hen:
"The way you bore me just won't do.
The way you laid me – all askew.
You barely kept me warm, and then
away you wandered, off you went
before I'd even hatched. How could you?"

Undated

Occasional and Joke Poems

From *An Anthology of Ancient Nonsense*

1. Jealousy

"Lesbia! Where have you been?" "In the arms of Morpheus."
"Don't lie to me, woman! I was in them myself!"

2.

The wind rips yellow leaves off the tops of the trees.
Lesbia! Over here! Look at all these fig-leaves!

3.

Phoebus? Gone for a spin in his golden chariot.
But he's due back tomorrow, by just the same route.

4.

The taps drown out the raucous voices, but you're the host…
"Oi! Run a bath if you want, not away from your guests!"

8.

"I love you!" he screamed for the thousandth time, and was done.
No doubt we'll hear him make it one thousand and one.

1911 – 1914

Baron Emil grabs a knife:
that damn pic's not true to life!
But Baron Emil, you've lost this one.
Baron Emil, the portrait's gone.

1914

[From Dmitri Shepelenko's album[56]]

No silk for us but only wool –
what a miserable tribe we are!
Hellish words keep our notebooks full.
Life sweats along, but doesn't get far.

Ascribed to Mandelstam

[To a writer]

As if some prophet down from talking with the Lord,
gibbering, you lumber towards your next award.

1920s (?)

Natasha's back, but where's she been?
She really must eat. She really must drink.
Dark as the night, her mother sniffs.
Her daughter reeks of onions and wine.

Early 1937

Oh Natasha, how clumsy of me
to not be Heinrich Heine.
Translating "knob", "sex yob" would be
my choice as rhyme designer.

Early 1937

Decision

If an Egyptian and me got hitched
under the pyramids' legal rules,
I'd buy my wife, my foreign match,
my lady friend, Pyramidon[57] pills.

We'd swim in the Nile and walk the temples,
in summer we'd take our picnic lunch
in the pyramids' shade, and I would fetch
my Lady of the Pyramids her pills.

March (?) 1937

Uncollected Poems

So if our enemies took me captive,
and no one squandered a word on me more,
and if they deprived me of all that I have,
the freedom to breathe, to push open a door,
to say once again that being should be
and declare it's the people's judgement that's judge,
if they dared to shackle me, like some wild beast,
and started to fling my feed on the floor,
I won't keep quiet or try to go numb,
but I'll draw the things that I'm free to draw,
and when I have swung the bare bell on its wall
and woken the hostile crowd in its corner,
I'll yoke ten oxen to my voice and bring down
my hand on that horde like a ploughshare,
and then, in the depths of the sentry's night,
the eyes of the brute-labouring earth will flare,
and into the dense legion of brotherly eyes
I'll fall with the heaviness of all harvests,
concise as a bale, oath racing away,
and the fiery years will land as a flock.
Lenin's ripe thunder is rustling past,
and here on the earth that escapes decay,
the life and thought of Stalin awakes.[58]

February 1937

Should I take charcoal for the highest praises,
for the sake of a joyful, unwavering drawing,
then taking care, as my body shakes,
I'd split the air up with ingenious corners.[59]
So life might find itself in those echoes,
this art that verges upon the audacious,
I'd speak of the man who moved the earth's axis,
observing one hundred and forty nations'
old ways. I'd raise a brow's least angle,
rethink it once I'd raised it some more.
Oh Prometheus blew on his flake of coal.
Aeschylus, look how I weep as I draw.

His thousand years bear no signs of ageing.
I'd gather a clutch of thundering lines,
with a smile on my face, I'd bind my courage,
turn it loose in some less loaded light.
And in that friendship of deep, wise eyes,
I won't say the name, but I'd find the words
to hint at that twin – the father you'll recognize,
choke as you sense how close the world is.
It's high time now that I thank the hills
that yielded this pencil, that grew this bone.
I won't call him Stalin, but Dzhugashvili,
who knew bitter prisons, is mountain-born.

Artist, protect and preserve the warrior.
Let a damp blue forest's growth defend him,
moist with vigilance. Cause him no worry
with arrears in ideas or an image unkind.
Artist, assist him, the one who's beside you,
who thinks and feels and builds. The people
are his and they are his Homer: neither
my nor your praises but theirs will triple.

Artist, protect and preserve this soldier
with his thickening forest of followers;
hearing him now ever louder and bolder,
even the future fights for that philosopher.

From the tribune's peak he leans over the mounds
of heads. This debtor outpowers all claims.
His eyes are decisive and kind, his brows
close on the face that they illuminate.
My compass needle could signal the way
to the father of resolute speeches, his lips;
labouring now from a million frames,
his craggy, sculpted, intricate eyelids.
Everything's open, judgement's copper:
no muted passages, hearing heightens.
His screwed-up, frowning wrinkles romp
over all those ready to commit their lives.

My ravenous hand gets the battlecall's gist,
as I clutch the stick where it all combines.
My clawing hand only hints at the axis;
I'll crumble the coal as I seek his guise.
I learn from him, but not on my behalf.
I learn from him, give myself no quarter.
Should accidents bury some subordinate part,
it's among their fumes his plan's to be sought.
Unworthy of friends, let me never be sated,
never be sated with bile and tears:
on the marvellous square, in his cap and greatcoat,
with his blissful eyes, once again he appears.

Those eyes have parted a mountain; a leviathan's
plough has furrowed a plain that's squinting
into the distance, the shining horizon,
tomorrow from yesterday, sea without wrinkles.
He smiles like a man with a sickle in hand
and harvests handshakes in bright conversation

which begins and continues without end
in that wide space where six oaths were taken.[60]
And every barn and every bale
is firm, wise, well-packed – these assets are living –
a people's miracle! Think large-scale!
Happiness spins and spins on this pivot.

Sluggish witness to struggle and harvest,
I'll hold his giant journey in my mind, sixfold,
until such time as that oath's discharged,
his route over taiga, through Lenin's October.
Moving off, the people's heads are hillocks.
No one can see me. My shape is tiny.
But in children's games, in affectionate books,
I'll rise once more and report on the sunshine.
No truth sparks truer than the honest knight's.
For air and steel, for honour and love
there's a name on the resolute lips of reciters,
a glorious name we've heard and discovered.

January – February (?) 1937

Biographical note

"What street are we on? / Mandelstam Street. / Damned if I know what that name means. / Try to unscrew it it still sounds wrong, / all twisted and not very clean."

None of Osip Mandelstam's groupings of poems can be quite resolved into something that exactly corresponds to today's notion of a stable, discrete collection. His first book, *Stone*, went through three differing editions (1913, 1916 and 1923): the first financed by Mandelstam's father; the second by the poet himself, substantially expanding the first but losing two poems to First World War Tsarist censorship; and the third also forming part of *Poems* (1928). The latter was a retrospective that included the poems of *Tristia*, originally published in Berlin in 1922 without Mandelstam's permission. An authorised (and censored) version of *Tristia* then appeared in the Soviet Union the following year under the title *The Second Book,* but the title reverted to *Tristia* in the 1928 retrospective, which in addition to *Stone* and *Tristia* included further poems written between 1921 and 1925.

A five-year silence ensued in terms of new poems, broken by a revival in Mandelstam's writing (but not publication) after his 1930 stay in Armenia. Nadezhda Mandelstam, the poet's wife, referred to these poems as the *Moscow Verses*, although several were written elsewhere, and A.G. Mets's edition prefers *New Verses* to designate these poems. They were followed from 1935 to 1937 by the three *Voronezh Notebooks*, the result of three separate renewed surges of poetic activity in internal exile. The conditions of their writing and preservation mean that these later poems in particular have been subject to considerable uncertainty regarding their ultimate text. With the exception of a very few poems from the *New Verses,* none of this later work was published in Mandelstam's lifetime.

Mandelstam was born into a Jewish family in Warsaw, then still part of the Russian Empire, in 1891. His retrospective prose piece *The Noise of Time* (1925) contrasts his mother's clear assimilation into Russian culture with his father's more ambivalent relationship to Russian and attachment to German literature and philosophy (though Clarence Brown, one of the first Western scholars to write on Mandelstam, suggests that Mandelstam overdramatised this contrast for literary effect). Osip moved with his family at an early age to St. Petersburg, where he attended the progressive Tenishev's School, whose alumni were also to include Vladimir Nabokov. At the age of twenty he converted to Methodism, principally to circumvent the restrictions then in place on Jews entering university, but the move was also emblematic of Mandelstam's affinity to the culture of Western Europe: Italian, German, French and Spanish poetry were all to become important to him. Anna Akhmatova, her then husband Nikolai Gumilyov and Mandelstam became the best-known members of the Acmeist school of poetry, which laid emphasis on the architectural quality of poetry and the meaning of the word "as such", in reaction to what they saw as the over-abstraction of Symbolist poetics, then in the ascendancy in Russia. Mandelstam wrote what would become the group's most famous manifesto, *The Morning of Acmeism,* though it was not published until some years after the group had established itself.

Mandelstam's politics have been the subject of critical contention. Youthful pre-war interest in the Social Revolutionaries, a rival leftist group to the Bolsheviks, transmuted to sympathy with Kerensky's Provisional Government that held power between the two Russian revolutions of 1917, tied to a suspicion of the incoming Bolsheviks and the means by which they were already establishing their hegemony. While in the Crimea for part of the Civil War that followed the October Revolution though, Mandelstam was equally dismayed by the violence of both Red and White forces. A recurring theme in iconic incidents related about Mandelstam is his insistent opposition to the death penalty. It remains debated as to what extent the absolute hostility to the Soviet authorities ascribed to him by his literary and political opponents during the 1920s and '30s was fully founded in fact. The period since the collapse of the Soviet Union has also seen it argued that his attitude to the Soviet state in the 1930s wavered between opposition and a desire to integrate himself back into Soviet life, and not only so as to save himself from the arrest and death he had long anticipated.

In any event, his work's admiration for the Classical and European past did not chime well with the Bolsheviks' emphasis on progress and the future (though with their conception of the poet as architect/builder, the Acmeists weren't quite as anti-modernist/progressive as their opponents made them out to be, despite Akhmatova and Gumilyov's aristocratic backgrounds). In the 1920s Mandelstam came under increasing pressure from writers and literary administrators more in line with the dominant political tendencies within the Soviet government. The second half of the 1920s saw him largely abandon poetry, in part at least through being told by Politburo member Nikolai Bukharin, later to die himself in Stalin's purges, that his poetry would no longer be published. Mandelstam's prose continued, however, and he supported himself by making literary translations chiefly from French as well as writing children's poetry.

Another recurring biographical trope is the ease with which Mandelstam would fall in love, whether or not this was requited. He had a relationship with the poet Marina Tsvetaeva for several months in 1916, and the evidence points to an infatuation with Akhmatova in the winter following the October Revolution of 1917. But the sturdiest anchor in his life was Nadezhda Mandelstam, née Khazina, whom he met in Kiev in 1919 and married three years later. She came to play an integral part in his poetry too, both in his lifetime and thereafter. Acting as his poetry secretary (Mandelstam's method of composition was primarily oral), she would then preserve his unpublished poetry after his death, in part through memorisation, enable its later publication after the Stalin era, and become a noted writer herself with her memoirs of life with Mandelstam and her subsequent odyssey through the Soviet Union.

Bukharin arranged in 1930 for Mandelstam to undertake an extended stay in the Caucasus, chiefly in Armenia. As well as the *Armenia* sequence translated here, the stay also resulted in the prose work *Journey to Armenia*, and prompted a second, if sporadic flourishing of Mandelstam's work (both poetry as well as his most extensive poetolgical essay, *Conversation on Dante*, of 1933). This later work, however, was to remain almost wholly unpublished in his lifetime. A poem openly critical of Stalin, translated here as *'We live, but feel no land at our feet'* and often referred to as "The Stalin Epigram", resulted in Mandelstam's first arrest after one of the few people he read the poem to – exactly who it was remains unknown – reported him to the NKVD (the Stalin-era name for what would later be known as the KGB). Following detention, interrogation and torture, Mandelstam was exiled first to the city of Cherdyn in the Urals (the journey to Cherdyn forms the background to the poem translated here as *The River Kama*), where he attempted to commit suicide by jumping from a third-floor window (his fall was broken by a bed of earth). Boris Pasternak, poet and later the author of the novel *Doctor Zhivago*, subsequently received a personal telephone call from Stalin, who asked Pasternak to provide an appraisal of Mandelstam. The brief intervention Pasternak was able to make may have played a part in Mandelstam being allowed to go into internal exile in a provincial city of his choosing. He chose Voronezh, 300 miles south of Moscow, in the fertile black earth region, adjacent to the Ukraine.

Finding a flat in Voronezh was as difficult as it had been previously in Moscow and Leningrad – at one point the Mandelstams were renting a balcony – but Osip was initially able to find occasional paid work with local cultural institutions such as the theatre and radio. But as Stalin's hold on power became ever tighter, gathering fear and repression meant that Osip and Nadezhda Mandelstam were largely ostracised and no longer able to find work in Voronezh, making their physical existence precarious. They were nevertheless befriended by the young school teacher Natasha Shtempel, to whom poems translated in this volume are addressed, and who was also to play a key role in the preservation of Mandelstam's work. Despite – or because of? – an ever-increasing sense of doom on Mandelstam's part, his poetic work proceeded apace, resulting in what have become known as the *Voronezh Notebooks*. These three notebooks survived the Stalin period variously through memorization and being hidden by several friends.

As with other Soviet poets of the period, Mandelstam made a more than understandable attempt to put himself on the right side of Stalin with the poem translated here as *'Should I take charcoal for the highest praises'*, which has become known as 'The Ode' (the fact that journals he submitted it to refused to publish it indicates just how dangerous his situation had become). As Mandelstam's work began to be circulated in samizdat form after Stalin's death, Nadezhda Mandelstam – again, understandably – chose to exclude this poem addressed to the man who had effectively murdered her husband from, if not the corpus, then the canon of Mandelstam's work, making much of the fact that the poem was drafted directly on paper rather than composed in his head as was Mandelstam's usual practice, indicating that the poem was composed under duress. Post-Soviet scholarship, however, such as that of M.L. Gasparov, has pointed to the poem's links and parallels with other poems Mandelstam was writing at the time, and while acknowledging the possible ironic, contradictory, subversive readings for the poem, argued that the poem cannot be reduced to simply a dissident interpretation.

In 1937, Mandelstam's term of internal exile in Voronezh ended. There followed a brief period of extreme nomadity in small towns around Moscow (from which Mandelstam himself was banned). A state-sponsored stay in a sanatorium allowed the authorities to isolate Mandelstam fully; from this sanatorium he was arrested and this time transported past the Urals and as far as a Gulag transit camp near Vladivostok in the Soviet Far East, where he died in late 1938. Famously, his widow received an official letter, via Mandelstam's brother, stating that her husband had died of "heart failure". For lack of details at the time, this was taken by her and the readers of her memoirs as being an evasion of specifying the real cause of death, and implying that he may have been shot. An eye-witness account of Mandelstam's actual death was to emerge in 1991, however: already severely weakened by a heart condition and malnutrition, Mandelstam had been standing unclothed for 40 minutes in freezing temperatures during a de-lousing action at the transit camp. He keeled over and died. It was, indeed, "heart failure".

Note on the poems

1. *Batyushkov,* Konstantin: 1787–1855, neoclassical poet.
2. *M.L. Lozinsky*: 1886–1955, poet, translator, close friend of Mandelstam, member of the proto-Acmeist "Guild of Poets", editor of the St. Petersburg journal *Hyperboria*, which published early work by Mandelstam.
3. Though the poem explicitly refers to Dickens' eponymous novel, its relationship to the novel's actual plot is tenuous: in the novel, Dombey's son dies as a child without working for his father, and Dombey does not attempt to commit suicide when he goes bankrupt.
4. *Valkyries*: from Old Norse *valkyrja*, "chooser of the slain". Figures from Scandinavian mythology whose tasks involved carrying slain warriors away from the battlefield to Valhalla. Richard Wagner's opera *The Valkyrie* was premiered in 1870. A manuscript version contains the bracketed title, omitted in *Stone*.
5. Mandelstam didn't like England very much.
6. *The Decembrist*: In the Decembrist revolt of 1825, liberal-minded officers and their troops refused to swear allegiance to the new tsar, Nicholas I. The revolt failed, and the tsarist authorities executed its leaders and exiled other participants to Siberia.
7. *Vera (Sudeikin)* (born Bosse, altered to de Bosset, Sudeikin at time of poem's writing, and later Stravinsky): 1888–1982, actress. *Serge Sudeikin*: 1882–1946, artist and set-designer.
8. *Taurida*: ancient Greek name for the Crimea.
9. *Meganom*: promontory on the south-east coast of the Crimea.
10. *asphodel*: In Homer's *Odyssey*, the Asphodel Meadows are the part of the Underworld where ordinary souls go after death.
11. *Soviet:* The 1928 retrospective *Poems* replaced this with 'January'; the poem was omitted entirely from the 1923 Soviet edition of *Tristia*, published as *The Second Book*.
12. *Cypris*: one of Aphrodite's names.
13. In the original, unauthorised edition of *Tristia* published in Berlin in 1922, lines 25 to 28 read:

    > Somewhere are the red ridges of the stalls,
    > luxurious boxes like fluffed-up wardrobes,
    > an officer walking like a clockwork doll –
    > no place for dark souls or the sanctimonious…

14. A draft version of the 1928 edition includes this stanza.
15. *Neaera*: name of various women and nymphs in Greek mythology.
16. *lapta*: Russian bat-and-ball game.

17. *The Ode on Slate*: The poem responds to lines written on a slate by Gavrila Derzhavin (1743–1816), just prior to his death:

>   Rushing onwards, time's river
>   Uproots all human things.
>   It drowns them all in oblivion:
>   Nations, kingdoms, kings.
>   Should some matter still survive
>   Among the lyres and pipes,
>   Like everything, it meets its fate,
>   Landing on eternity's plate.

18. In 1937, Mandelstam deleted these eight lines in square brackets by hand in a copy of the 1928 edition, placing the fifth and sixth lines as an epigraph to the poem.
19. *the bustard's anger*: "the male Little Bustard has a flamboyant display with foot stamping and leaping in the air" (Wikipedia).
20. Cf. the churchyard scene in Hamlet, Act V, Scene 1: "What is he that builds stronger than either the mason, the shipwright, or the carpenter?" (1st Clown)
21. These prefatory lines were censored in the cycle's 1931 publication in the journal *Novy Mir*, according to Nadezhda Mandelstam.
22. *ocarina:* ancient wind instrument comprising an enclosed space and a number of holes, variants of which can be found in various cultures across the world.
23. *dudka*: Russianized hearing of *duduk*, an Armenian double-reed wind instrument.
24. A censored version of this poem was published in a journal in 1932 under the title 'Leningrad', by which the poem has become known. The 'Vatican Codex' of final, authorised texts later prepared by the Mandelstams does not include a title for this poem.
25. *escheated*: reverting to the state in the absence of legal heirs.
26. *medulla oblongata*: cone-shaped neuronal mass located in the human hindbrain, responsible for involuntary actions such as vomiting and sneezing.
27. *B.C. Kuzin*: 1903–1975, entomologist/biologist and neo-Lamarckian whom Mandelstam met and befriended in Armenia; a fan of Goethe and Bach, but not, according to Nadezhda Mandelstam, of this poem.
28. "Friend, don't miss out on life: / the years fly on, / and the juice from the vines / won't warm us for long." Included in some manuscripts.
29. *Ewald Christian Kleist*: 1715–1759, German poet and Prussian officer who died fighting the Russians at the Battle of Kunersdorf during the Seven Years' War.

30. *Ceres*: Roman goddess of agriculture, fertility and marriage.
31. *Pylades*: in Greek mythology and plays, friend, perhaps lover, of Orestes. Assisted the latter in various tangles with the Gods; didn't talk a lot.
32. *lemon*: The original's "raspberry" is Russian thieves' cant for the criminal underworld. The translation here has acultural recourse to Cockney rhyming slang.
33. *Ivan the Steward*: hero of Russian folk songs, including *Kak v slavnom bylo v Moskvye gorodye* (loosely, How Glory Came to Moscow Town), in which he is executed by the Prince for having an affair with the Princess.
34. *vin d'Ay*: champagne brand.
35. This four-liner is one of the Eigers of Mandelstam translation. In the spirit of Mandelstam's own willingness to preserve variants of his later poems, an alternative route is offered here in italics.
36. *land and liberty*: refers to the 1870s Russian revolutionary organization *Zemlya i volya* (Land and Liberty), whose 1879 congress was in Voronezh.
37. *Ob, Tobol*: rivers in Western Siberia and Kazakhstan/Urals respectively. Mets suggests that these were the names of boats observed by Mandelstam on the river journey related in the poem.
38. Nadezhda Mandelstam describes this as a version for the censor, stating that her husband saw it as an independent section of the poem. Mets deletes this second version on the basis of the manuscripts and notes from Mandelstam's lifetime.
39. Shortly before this poem was written, the Soviet Union's criminal code was amended to apply to juveniles down to the age of 12, who thereby became subject to criminal courts and all punishments then on the statutes, including capital punishment.
40. Originally the third stanza of a draft poem whose first and second stanzas read:

>   It smiles and chews the choicest seed,
>   its mouth like that of a child.
>   Golden boy, I cock my head
>   and catch that hopping gold.
>
>   You're so goldfinch. The plumage sewed
>   below your beak is reddish.
>   The goldfinch kind. Your tail's a boat,
>   yellow and black your feathers.

41. *cochineal*: scarlet dye from a Mexican insect.
42. Original draft of a poem subsequently revised radically, parts of which appear as separate poems at this point in the *Second Notebook* in the Mets edition.

43. According to Nadezhda Mandelstam, this image derives from a map of the Voronezh region at the telephone exchange showing which connections were currently available for the waiting callers.
44. *Anna, Rossosh, Gremachye*: settlements in the Voronezh region.
45. *Koltsov*, Aleksey: 1809–1842, Russian poet, some of whose work consisted in stylized peasant songs, born and died in Voronezh.
46. *Salamanca*: Mandelstam began learning Spanish in late 1936 and became interested in Luis de Léon (1527–1591), poet and professor at the University of Salamanca, who spent many years in the dungeons of the Inquisition. Another possible reference is to Miguel de Unamuno (1864–1936), poet and rector of the University of Salamanca, dismissed by Franco for a speech critical of the Spanish fascist mutiny.
47. *open city*: city in wartime that is no longer defended but declared open to an advancing enemy.
48. *blackdamp*: mixture of gases left once oxygen has been removed from the air, an asphyxiant and mining hazard.
49. The exact text of this poem, available only in various manuscript stages, has been subject to debate. This translation essentially follows the Mets edition, while retaining a section (2a) that Mets drops.
50. *Lermontov*, Mikhail: 1814–1841, Russian poet, though best known outside of Russia for his formally innovative short novel *A Hero of Our Time*.
51. *berry, ah*: The original here is "yagoda", berry, but also referring to Genrikh Yagoda, head of the NKVD from 1934 to 1936 and himself arrested in March 1937. Slightly anachronistically, the translation replaces the pun on Yagoda with one on Lavrentiy Beria, who did not become head of the NKVD until November 1938, after the writing of this poem and shortly before Mandelstam's death.
52. *Švejk*: main figure in the Czech writer Jaroslav Hašek's unfinished satirical novel of the First World War *The Good Soldier Švejk*.
53. *Reims, Laon*: French towns famous for their respective Gothic cathedrals, both of them "Notre Dames" like the cathedral in Paris from which Mandelstam's earlier poem in *Stone* took its name. The title of this later poem is given in a manuscript in the Princeton archive of Mandelstam's poems, but omitted in the Mets edition.
54. The text of this poem too is disputed. As Richard and Elizabeth McKane point out, and mentioned in Nerler's notes, Nadezhda Mandelstam considered the basic poem to consist only in the two stanzas translated here as stanzas II and V. Both Mets and Nerler keep the entire text, however. According to Nadezhda Mandelstam, the poem acquired a political meaning after the 1937 arrest of the Voronezh flautist Carl Schwab on false charges of spying. Is it possible, perhaps, to hear the sound of a flute in the first stanza? Like Mandelstam, Schwab died in the gulags in 1938. The poem was written down in code.

55. On first reading this poem to its dedicatee, Mandelstam told Shtempel that she should see to it that it was preserved in the Pushkin House, the archive of Russian literature, in (then) Leningrad, as it was his best poem. The latter statement may have been a belated atonement for an incident Shtempel related to Mandelstam scholar Clarence Brown in Moscow in 1966. On first meeting Mandelstam in Voronezh, she had expressed her admiration for his poetry. He asked her to recite a poem of his, and she obliged with a piece of Mandelstam's occasional verse from 1916, about a lost amulet. Mandelstam shouted at her saying that this was his worst poem and that she was to leave him alone.
56. *Dmitri Shepelenko*: 1897–1972, Russian poet, member of the Tbilisi Guild of Poets, and Mandelstam's neighbour in the Herzen House, Moscow, from 1922 to 1924.
57. *Pyramidon*®: tradename of the drug Aminophenazon; due to carcinogenic effects, now no longer prescribed.
58. A variant of this line could be translated as "The life and thought of Stalin lays waste." Mets regards this as self-parody on the poet's part, disagreeing with Nadezhda Mandelstam's view of it as a non-self-censored version that should take priority.
59. *ingenious corners:* Nerler suggests that this might refer to sketch-artists' practice of copying portraits in sections by setting out squares with a ruler.
60. *where six oaths were taken*: This refers to six "oaths" taken by Stalin, pledging to uphold Lenin's precepts, in a speech at Lenin's funeral on 26 January 1924 (according to Nerler) or at the 2nd All Union Congress of Soviets convened after Lenin's death (according to Mets).

www.ingramcontent.com/pod-product-compliance
Lightning Source LLC
Chambersburg PA
CBHW031151160426
43193CB00008B/327